Spells for Clear Vision

June Suckling, May Day 1919, Lake Forest, Illinois

Neile Graham
Spells for Clear Vision

Neile Graham (signature)

Brick Books

CANADIAN CATALOGUING IN PUBLICATION DATA

Graham, Neile
    Spells for clear vision

Poems.
ISBN 0-919626-74-2

1. Title.

PS8563.R323S74 1994   C811'.54   C94-932639-9
PR9199.3.G73S74 1994

The support of the Canada Council and the Ontario Arts Council
is gratefully acknowledged. The support of the Government of
Ontario through the Ministry of Culture, Tourism and Recreation
is also gratefully acknowledged.

Cover is after a painting by Alison Skelton.
Author photo by Gail L. Dubrow.

Typeset in Ehrhardt. Printed and bound by The Porcupine's Quill.
The stock is acid-free Zephyr Antique laid.

Brick Books
431 Boler Road, Box 20081
London, Ontario
N6K 4G6

This book is for Jim:
spells for the temple

CONTENTS

1. The Grass She Stands In

'Sometimes I wish someone reliable would tuck
me into bed and tell me the story of my life.'

William S. Wilson, *Birthplace*

This is the gift my mother gives –
a hint of vision, chunk of glass
tongued and ground by waves,

tossed onto the rock by
winter tides. This
my mother sees; having walked

across the mudflats to the remains
of Ohiat village to Execution Rock,
she finds this bit of green

with the taste of ocean, some white
man's bottle turned into beauty
by sand and time.

Another gift, the tale of her journey.
She writes *Last night was special dark,*
dark with all possible stars,

the milky way and quiet.
We were out in a herring skiff
admiring bioluminescence trailing

from paddles and dip nets....
Stars above and below!
I told her I'd steal those words

to trade for what I cannot see
in the city except a hint that rides
in with winds from the Sound, a rumour

that brings the ocean here.
The cedars outside my door shake it for news,
and I stand outside in dim winter rain

on my way to work, guess at the meaning
of the weaving branches, the taste
of salt air, touch the bit of glass

in my pocket to see the cloud-hidden stars,
the falling rain catching sparks from streetlights
to scatter on the streets below.

The wind tonight is not quite spring but holds
a fragrant hint of soil, and blind shoots
wake to that scent.
                              In gusts at once warm and cool
there is no room for bare feet or women like white birds
in Grecian gowns. It's not yet May and sixty-five years
have spun by. She's dead, who in this photograph presses
naked feet against grass, raises arms to dance,
a white shawl drifting like feathers from her hands.
She knows nothing yet. Her confidence, tender
as a bird's.
                    I can't trust the web spun between us
to bind her, it's stretched over so many years.
Looking at this girl, I wonder how much I would explain to her,
how I could warn her that her first child will be still-born.
Defying the doctor to conceive another, she'll take a pin
to the French safe he made her husband wear. Her daughter
will bear me and I will remember her old in the mahogany bed
lying in regal darkness at the curving hall's end,
never dreaming of this white-gowned girl with waist-long hair
stepping into the history of her life

and mine. The wind pushing through her to me
is fecund with dreams and mud and doesn't tie us. Each movement
I make toward her is another step in her dance, another breath
of wind pressing her forward into the season.
                                        I remember gathering
her sweeping hair into a widow's bun. Her hair still dark as
distance, yet light as birds and the girl I create of her.

Running from the Palace Hotel
holding her mother's hand
is all she remembers, nothing
of what she must have seen.
At five that morning the walls
began rattling the city awake,
tenements were flattened,
and hospitals closed.
Only six years old,
my grandmother. She
and Caruso at the same grand hotel
shaken out into the shifting streets.
Only history describes what
went on around her.
At nine the ham-and-eggs
fire began: someone cooking
over his familiar stove
when the broken chimney caught –
with quake-snapped lines
there was no water
and a city in flames. Looting
soldiers, dance halls
turned to hospitals for shattered
survivors, someone telegraphing
fire-and-destruction
to a world outside,
buildings exploded in the path
of the fire, the sun
red with dust, smoke
and fear. No communication.
At three-thirty the hotel bartenders
gave away the wine from the cellars.
By five that evening
the hotel was gone.
Where in the streets

would they have found haven?
Did they sleep in a park
nights after the Palace Hotel?
What did they lose there?
How did they return
to their Manitoba town
and what were the stories
they could have told
to pay their way home,
by sea, by train, the incidents
that made up their history?
How shock must have
faded to silence, human memory
as tenuous a lifeline
as a child on the streets
clinging to her mother's warm hand,
the silence sudden around them.

Sea wind runs into the strait
                    like salmon
quicksilver
            and cold in late spring.
On the dock outside the small motel

my mother sits alone –
                    sun up,
fishing boats head into the current
a foghorn hums from the strait's other shore.

The rocky seaweed
                    steams in the light.

Last night they feasted
                    on salmon at Hoback Beach
and a Makah elder traded drums with her.

He took the one made of the hide
she had stretched and sewn,
that her Kwagulth friend painted

with Thunderbird
                    turning human, tongue outstretched

and he started drumming and chanting.
He gave her his own and told her to drum.

So there she was
                    drumming
while the others chanted
to invite the people to eat.

He said her drum had good tone
and she should use it lots, told her
                    a story

about the eagle and lightning snakes
on the drum he loaned her.

Sea spray tightens
                    the skin on her face
while the morning sun
                    splinters
on the white caps. My mother still drums

on Hoback Beach following
the lead of the man drumming
on what she has made –
                    teaching her
the chants in a tongue that
    as she learns it
                    becomes her own.

He steps away from the chattering tourists,
out of the sun, the heat, the bright day,
leaves my mother resting in the shade just under
the jungle's edge. Ducking his head beneath
the low stones of the arch, he steps into darkness
the musty smell of centuries, of grit and splintering
stone, and breathes it in: the room
he has waited his life to enter. The room
where – the instant his shadow breaks the light
against the far wall – the feathered priest
and the sweating stoneworker breathe
into his open mouth and back away,
a sour taste that my father,
for that moment, knows.
But his shadow is still moving, and there's
the light again, whole against the wall;
shaking his heat-weary head
he bends out again. The two strangers
flicker once behind him and are
gone. Out in the thick sun, he rests his hand
lightly on the broken curve of the jutting
stone above him, not certain what it is
he now knows, but a man's height is nothing,
and something, despite the years he wears,
despite the unaccustomed heat, drives him,
fills him with the urge to climb the mound,
and climb he does, his sweat binding
the shirt to his skin, he steps higher,
thinking only of the strength that carries
him, the blood pumping strong through his heart
and legs, the muscles he can still trust, higher
till he reaches the top and turns
to see the path he's taken here,
the crumbling stones bound with grass,
the other mounds, the dark doorway hidden below,

and my mother, holding one hand above her eyes,
waving the other, the sea of green trees stretching
out before him, rich and ragged and warring
as the breath rasping in and out of his tired lungs.
He rests his hands on his strong shaking legs,
looks out and out over this land, these trees
the stones beneath his feet and the ones
who know him.

for Christine MacDougall

I hang the Thunderbird your son carved
next to my door

to say I know you
and what belongs to your people
mine can only borrow.
I hope not to abuse what we have taken

but hope is worth little
and pains me until even my guilt

isn't honest – the carving is small
but cedar
and richly stained.
It is somehow warm.

In the city where I live
a museum bought the house you grew up in.

To enter the proper silence
of your home
you must weave through
crowds of children at play

with tricks, the bright, loud games
of science, modern white magic.

The panels there call your uncle
chief, though
that was your father's place;
their words don't say

what your uncle did with the money they paid
for selling a home not his alone.

Inside I wondered how those transplanted
walls were when your family
breathed this place alive, the sounds
of shore birds, the tang of sea and forest,

how these cedar planks held your days,
held the first words you spoke –

then how it must have been for you
to enter it yourself, here. I only know I can't know
what you thought about the word we call *home*.
You live on an island with Salmon

and Cedar – who tell no lies.
And my rhetoric falls nowhere between us,

so I offer you a space in my house,
the honest affection behind my mask of words.
I place your son's carving
where I see it just as I leave my home

to remind me each time of the poverty
and riches of the world I step out into.

FIVE CROW PHOTOGRAPHS

after the photographs of Fred E. Miller

1   *Crow Girl on Prairie in Elk's Tooth Dress*

So young and straight, this girl,
frowning a little into summer sun.
A child with a face clear and wise.
Her shadow thrusts out behind her
into the plains, as though
she might abandon the dirt field,
turn and run that direction,
off into the rest of her life.
Yet she stands in that dress, proud
and simple; its elk's teeth gleam,
pointing white to the ground her feet
know so well, the ground which
lifts her in any direction she'll run.

A thin line of horses and tipis
mark out the ground behind him. Two
horses graze nearer, and closer still
a stake and a tether. These
are all he has at hand.
But it's enough for him –
maybe six years old
he stands like a man, his legs
a little splayed and strong.
He has what he needs, his gear.
The paint strip across his nose and cheeks
isn't just for show.
In an earlier day it would not be
the camera he faces so boldly
but instead his future: counting coup
against the Blackfeet, stealing horses
to call his own. But still
Aloysius Holds The Enemy tight against the palm
of his defiant fist.
He could crush them. He knows.

3 *Crow Girl*

Someone must remember her name,
this girl who fills the land surrounding her.
It is certain she does. Though they're hidden
under the blanket wrapped around her,
she has sure hands. She knows this plain,
has made it into herself. It shapes her
like the grass she stands in:
blades drying, it readies itself for
snow. Rising like the white man's house
behind her, but steady and lasting
as the earth beneath her hidden feet.

4 *Crow Girls Decorating Graves at Custer Battlefield
on the 25th Anniversary, June 25, 1901*

Around them, the plain.
Light cuts it, makes clear the division
between each blade of prairie grass, each stone.
Behind them the light is naked
on the fields they've crossed, on
the beams of loose grass they've
pushed aside. If they listen,
they hear the rustling of angry sun
grain stuck in its throat.
They've walked too far not to know
the place where they stumble
the harsh breath they turn into
waiting in June heat.
Summer and they stand gathered in the battlefield
around them the earth
breaking with light.

5 *Four-Pole Crow Burial Scaffold; A Hillside in Spring*

So empty at first: this human structure
poised against the rise of the plains,
the hill straight across the skyline
like the edge of the world.
Openness so final and framed.
The white cloth that tops the scaffold
seals itself and the angles beneath it,
and nothing dares breathe. Yet
the scaffold's shadow creeps across the grasses,
an animal stepping home, moves
like the season's wind must, lightly
and without fear. The wildflowers push up,
their heads furious with sun,
until the cloth that lifts the body
into the air is full, and the hill
is the earth's back bending
as it bows to the sky.

POSTCARD OF O'KEEFFE

A raven of a woman,
black wings stark

as the one upturned
face in a crowd –

surrounded by anything –
she emerges from the dark

weight of her clothes.
She denies herself colour

so in her work she may use it
to overcome the world's light.

There is nothing
she cannot claim: the wash

of a desert, golden to red,
sun-cleansed bones that could

line the hill's back, the spread
of sky or an offering flower

more open than her watching eyes.
How the sun burns in all its

persuasions.... All this pours
from her strong, round frame,

more knowledge than it can
bear – the shadows of the world

that she lets bear her down;
the light that flows from her hands.

Berlin sleeps under soot under snow
under pure cold, and something wakes
you, the children stirring in your womb,
perhaps your own thumping heart
or the stubborn ache in the hollow of your back.
Walk to the kitchen, pour yourself
a glass of cool water sipping it
as you gaze out the window wondering how
you came to be here this hour of the night
in an older foreign land even now still
divided into twins like those you carry
so heavily in your belly. Strange to believe
you will soon touch and kiss
the limbs that now push against your fingers
as you trace their shape through your skin.
You dream of those children in the half winter
of this night and wonder what your husband dreams of
so solid and soundly asleep back under the quilts
while the life in you moves and twists,
restless as winter birds. You think of the night,
how it opens and stretches back to your home,
the moon now lighting the dusky snow into a wakening
brightness, your quiet self watching the empty streets,
watching yourself from the far window, watching always
those two small bodies dreaming under
the warm thunder of your heart.

for John Barton

Everything on the street leaned
against us. The squalid hot
urine smell of the city, the traffic
and sirens shouting violence and waste,
the museums full of anguish and beauty.
I couldn't make sense of it,
could feel all those lives
burning, beginning.

Wiping sweat off my throat
all night at the Y. Naked,
restless, in the gritty dark
roach-crawling room.
The simplest distinctions
began to blur. I saw Eva Hesse's
fibreglass boxes perched uneasily
holding nothing. Nevelson's
Dawn's White Wedding Chapel,
cool, labyrinthine. The man
on the street with the bleeding hand.

At last I saw I couldn't put
anything into those boxes.

We took the wrong subway, stepped
out into a vacant air
a woman told us was Harlem.
It was quiet there.
As we walked through the streets
toward Needle Park, I couldn't understand
the word *ghetto*
and what it didn't mean that morning.

The emptied streets, the park
and the trees where a man
walked his dogs in the last days
of summer, the two men
on the stairs as we passed,
who hardly glanced at our edgy flight.

Caught in a storm that night
in the Village, we sat in a restaurant,
talked ourselves tired –
and it wasn't just lightning
turning the night sky to fire
that cracked open our lives.
It was the layers of dust
that wouldn't wash from my skin.
Godard's *Breathless* in the
dank theatre. *Starry Night's*
thick pigments behind heavy glass, each
brushstroke an etching
of open desire. The few birds
in Needle Park chattering
in the green heat. Rain falling
like it could scrub the streets clean.

This is my pack, a bud that closes
around everything I own. At the centre
its heart, my life. When I
open it, my hands savour
the warmth that rushes from it like waves.
Inside I find my sandpaper towel
to strip the damp from my skin. Insect shell
sandals to guard my feet from gravel and heat,
scars of the lake's shifting. A tin cup
so I can swallow the water that
swallows me. My notebook to fan
the lake's rain from my face.
My pen to etch my name
on the cup and in the pages of my book.
This is my pack, my pillow against the world.
This is my book, my blanket.

I call it sorrow that makes me leave
this house; unfolding the cloth that covers
the windows, I am closing the eyes of the dead.
It's grey, raining outside and it suits me well,
pulling the door to, turning the key in the familiar
lock one last time.
                              This time I forgot to say
goodbye to each room, like I did as a child,
so I step through the soggy leaves and circle
the house trying to make it whole.

If I knew the words to make the sort
of spell this needs I would say them. Instead I walk
to the car, try not to look back.

Suddenly I'm miles away in the rain
on the highway and can't remember how
I got this far; the windshield wipers
scrape in front of my eyes and I'm driving inland –
away from the land's end,
from the house at the edge of it.

If I stare out the attic window at the night sea
I cannot quite make out where shore ends
and ocean begins: the limits of everything
undone in darkness just as on the highway
grey road dissolves to grey sky.

I am leaving nothing, take the weight of my life
down this road, though I thought I had left
it behind. Sorrow, like darkness, like rain,
blurs all borders and everything comes flooding in –

I greet each room like a child.

II.   The Weight of Clear Water

'It would be worth something to go toward a star
that is a lamp in the mountains,' said Bobi,
'that's all.'

Jean Giono, *Joy of Man's Desiring*

In winter you are the first thing that freezes
in the space between word and word,
between branch and twig where the leaves
were lost in the first deep frost.
We walk by the river, where
ice forms halos around stones.
You say *south* like an old man
dimly holding to one thing he knows.

I'd rather say *Canada, home,* whose
name is the sound of ice cracking
and the bird's call across snow.
I want to name the gap between us;
we pad it with words, old sweaters
to keep out chill, watch the river
moving someplace we never go, south, where
like new leaves your hands will open.

In the thin edge of greying sky
snow twists
            over the mountain like gauze
snaps
        on the pines, thickens
in the glazed crevasses
                    stirs the scree
like a machine of wind.
The raw night air
                is ice itself.
It is restless, still dark.

We shake the blown snow
from our clothes, keep moving
cutting through all that
                    dawn edging
over the side of the ridge
into the weeds and river
the effortless snow
                falling on snow.
We have no direction
                    but out into the air
taking it in so deeply
it fills us
        wiping ice
over our sweating faces
the taste of clean snowfall.

Blowing snow turns to water
against our warm skin.
                    Bare wind
through the birches disturbs
what might have been
                    rustling leaves
but not there.

                    We walk
across the fallen pine
jump over the ice blowing
around the rocks of the stream, break
off a piece
                    to place on our tongues.

We'd find a burrow
dry and dull with earth
scramble down
                    beneath thatched roots
to the nest
of last fall's grasses
                            but no:
wind weaves moss
in the high old branches
like the *whish* of birds
                            shifting their wings
before sleeping, the sigh
of night settling
                    into its vibrant bed
curled and wintering.

This is the beginning
of the sun's slow crawl
out over the mountains till
it
    breaks over the valley
and stands amazed,
                    daylight like blood
spreading
            on the snow. If
we believe in anything
it is this.

Sky naked as flesh. The air
cracked and cold as stone
chipped like obsidian
into a cunning blade.
These days strip you
till you're raw as a man
who sees just one direction,
and you hold the wind
like ice till it melts
in your hand. The river's
skin peels and flakes,
the river bleeds
mud from the hills.
Light pours from your flesh:
a scarce, fertile rain.
Clouds darken and shuffle in
from the east. And now
the night is a bear,
his bulk a shy eclipse.
Near morning his fur
is black, clear as obsidian,
his purpose never blunted.
Wind shaves your hands.

BIRD AT DAYBREAK

for Jim

Light cuts through
the gap between blind
and window frame
to my palm.
Burning I say,
burning you repeat
in your sleep, then
turn to lie closer
against me. I hold
the light in my hand
like a bird – it beats
with blood and flight.
I can't move my arm
or close my fingers,
can't wake you.
The bird spreads its wings
as I try to call
your name, settles
when my voice won't rise
from my throat.
The bird and I burn
like sun,
like morning.
You're still in night:
fighting your way
through layers of sleep,
you speak my name.
I stare at my hand.
The bird burns deeper
as your eyes open
and you touch my open hand.

1 Your face never so open
your warm cheek against mine
and my breath hidden against
your shoulder – this is that pain
that I cannot rest on cannot
sleep in. Even in our lives
so ordinary they almost
disappear without us.
The wind at the door blowing
the scudding clouds in –
another chance to prove that
this moment is true. That
my hand resting on your hair
is love. Summer is outside, discarded
yet the sun falls on everything,
equally. On the fat tomatoes
and the drying grasses, the wasp above
the wisp of a flower, the husk of the pod.
The lonely dog barks next door and the boys
yell at the football game. The laundry
dried hours ago still waits on the line.
Summer survives all this, survives September.
Lives out the early darkness, the night chill,
the heavy moon pulling it away. Clings,
loosens its hold, comes back.
The cat chatters at a bug on the
wrong side of the window. It
cheated her. She wants outside
in the sun, wants to chase
all the flies into the first frost.
Wants to chase the leaves that
aren't yet falling.

2 The fat moon, almost full, skims the ridges
  of the firs, pulling the hill higher.
  Just past the autumnal equinox,
  the usual storms have skipped this shore;
  the wind is still balmy
  and hasn't yet heralded hard rain.
  So lazy a wind spins out summer
  like a twisted thread of yarn, drawing
  it out ever longer and we haven't found
  its end yet. It will be a sudden knot
  when it comes. Banging at its heels will be rain.
  Now the flowers fool themselves into
  blooming again, fearless as angels.
  Can't blame them, this summer seems
  as endless as the ocean, more days to it
  than waves landing on the rocks
  below us. I sit on a log watching
  them there, caught in a net of stories
  you tell, stories about summers like these
  when you were a boy, weather that turned
  or did not turn, the humid sun
  and the sullen southern heat that's here.

3 Nightblind at the window: this is my one chance
   to lose everything. I slip out of bed on waking
   and the floor numbs my feet. Outside the window
   I can't see a thing, I can believe
   it is no longer there – the house around me
   and all the shadows there
   are hidden by the absence outside
   and my slowly waking mind. I feel
   almost free. If I believe my eyes
   I am in the most open place I will ever be;
   nothing surrounds me. I have only
   what I want to remember and the space
   spreads before me, I can breathe my way
   farther across miles of this place
   to a place just the same and no less open.
   My limbs are light and naked and nothing
   is ever the same. The wind on my arms
   smells of salt and hollow grass and of
   never stopping. Any direction I am moving
   is forward. My own breath turns to loam
   and to laughter, growing at my feet and
   placing me here, leaning spread against
   the cold plate of the window glass, willing
   to lose it all for the chance to be swallowed by
   that sky out there, blacker than midnight,
   black with neither moon nor star.

4   The weariness of my bones is lifted
and settles deeper in. I can open it like a
gate and walk through – it's a stone, a door,
a promise and goodbye: if I held it in my hands,
if I could hold it, it would thrum with
heartbeat, hidden song. The world comes in
the real one tasting of salt and ashes,
spice and dust. The air still thick
with heat.

5   Clouds dark as ocean, as fear,
    hang above the forest. The storm
    knots inside them. I stand on the rock knoll
    above the waterfall of moss and wild grasses
    that tumbles down the hillside,
    waiting for the wind: and the first
    thick fall of rain beads on my face, tears
    down. Then the wind comes –
    a familiar, angry stranger – I lean into it
    wave after wave holds me then lets go
    disappears and calls the branches after.
    Like leashed dogs they keep trying to go.
    An eddy of rain spins around me
    twigs hit, then stick to, my skin. Each gust
    of the storm is precious to me. Its wild dance
    I rise into – dangerous stranger –
    strong unknowable so lovable one, its arms
    everywhere, nowhere, the one man unpreventable
    alive with cause, alive despite us, to spite us,
    this dark, cold, and dancing man
    I would take as a lover takes me.

6 And it's gone.
  This tree in this late afternoon clouded white
  sunlight, this needle fallen from it in my hand.
  One end crushed by my fingers, the scent
  shining from it like a match's flare.
  So – I call it here from my mind's
  file of places. Here into this house
  I brought it, felt that needle in my palm
  and smelled it better
  than the word *forest*. Stole it and
  brought it here. Hoarder. Ferreter away of
  cones and stones, surf pebbles and beach
  glass to put in my hand on my tongue
  to make it speak.

hot wind came from the marshes
through air thick with
rotting weeds we wade   fish
from the spawning steam
in Indian summer, in red
leafed shrouds   fleshy anchors
our legs weigh us into the mud

death-chill from the mountains
we reach the rock   begin to climb
an old stream-bed crevassed
between mountains shedding
shale and scree that runs past us
in waves

a leaf in the current
pushing ourselves the wrong direction
leaving the marsh for these awkward
heights, our hands fall away
from each other   bands of chill air
tumble down the slopes

but the eyes and stance between the eyes
but the sun's warmth still pushes us
higher   here is a place
we can turn and look before us
distance spreads the air
where currents of
winter and summer meet
in the winds   exchange

casting but shade beyond the other lights
love   this is not beauty
but trial   the sun
not setting but distant

we wait for the stars to fade in
to brighten us   waiting

sky's clear / night's sea / green of the mountain pool
and now sky is water   but clear
and we breathe it to fill ourselves
the pattern below us
darkening   the wind settles to frost
hands held   without touching

HERO AT THE GATES OF HELL

for Bette Tomlinson

I'm afraid to ask the right questions.
The ones that elicit instruction and
guidance: how to hold a tree against
weather, my hands against time.
If only I hadn't come to this,
seen how shadows hold a greater light
across the darkness. No one will believe me.
And when I return I will invest everything
with strange new qualities.
The morning sun will brighten my room
in a way that will seem new, and when
I wake to it, leave my bed
and cross the cool floor to hold
the pitcher, feel the good clay
and its weight of clear water,
I will think how the moment
is so beautiful no one
would ever know it's not perfect.

iii.   The Tree Bursting Alive

'There's two things that charm the eyes
like wizardry. One's flames, but flames
I've seen enough to last my life. The
other's water. I watch that river
till I think I even hear him sing.'

Frederick Buechner, *Godric*

Presented by the Queen's
Printer, this map excises
something north.
Somewhere west as well,
you can tell because

east of both island and strait
the mainland stretches toward
and beyond the margins.
The island itself is far
paler green and brown

than anyone could imagine
an island being. The highways
are red, which no tourist
ever reported seeing on
the main asphalt lines,

perhaps to represent the way
the roads all stop
short at water's edge,
an unofficial warning.
The sea itself is a flat,

soft blue, like January
sky. No whitecaps.
No sailboats or gale warnings.
Dotted lines direct
the ferries. All

along the western coast,
areas in which many shipwrecks
have occurred are indicated
thus (a black three-masted schooner
going down).

Summer's end. Wild flowers
dry and fall to weeds, brown-gold mats

that drift around my feet while the winds
step up the slope of the ridge

to tumble down the leeside, spilling rain.
The city mumbles: crows itch, sirens wind,

children laugh and battle, traffic
and a hammer's echo, a door's slam,

someone yells *no*. Wind like hands on my face,
chill and alive, knots rain into the bushes,

over grasses, into the sky and beyond.
I want to follow there, drink the clear

stream's water away from the hiss of cars.
The pure cold sky burning in my lungs

and the ache of muscle used well
where the winds meet in their wheeling dance.

Two cedars outside my window replace
what is not now the forest; they're sanctuary

for small birds who remain in the city,
haven for squirrels, something left

to hold the wind. And when we are sleeping,
our faces washed in the city's unnatural light,

the wind in the cedars sounds
like a forest, seedlings find soil

in cracks of the pavement
life enough to call this place home.

The thin edge of something alive
in the blunting darkness, green shoots

in a line of soil and the twist of rain
sprung against my face, retreating again

into the warm hollow where the wind doesn't go.
The branches beat against our window,

sound like magic from our bed.

What is the poison
named? We are the ones
who would name it madness.
What light comes out of
the covered sky that makes
the pines shine like
this? – This is what
we should ask. We should
tell stories, clear and true
that equal what we would say
but it isn't that simple.
What light makes the trees
so green on such a dark day?

———

Our shoes stick in the mud.
The red-gold dog runs ahead
of us, runs behind, his mane
brambled with pine and twigs.
Your fingers are cold
when they touch mine.
The sky grey through and through.
As the light thins within the ravine
the trees lean up the banks
where they can. Mist collects
and falls from the tips of
branches like an offering
to a thirsting god. It
could be us, we could live
on this distilled breath
of fir. The plaid of your
shirt in front of me takes
me home, and I recall
how this morning, not speaking,
you stretched it over
your brown shoulders and turned

away. It isn't much, this
sharing. We keep walking
down into the dark ravine
and I begin to walk slower
fall behind till I feel
alone in this thicket and
it rises so green around
me, shoots into the sky,
however grey. Bursting above me.

———

Step out, and you're waiting.
The dog offers us each an
end of his stick and we take
it and smile. You think I tell
this story to create itself. You think
I say these things to make them
true.

SALTSPRING

for Brenda Ireland

Early island light
with characters: the heron
skimming from rock to rock, just off shore;
the crows that led me far down the beach
taunting me farther; the sea itself, coming in;
my friend inside, sleeping; the gulls; the terns;
the river otters who bobbed their heads
over the log below me; the last otter, hesitant, stared.

Light with objects: the shells
perfect but still inhabited; plants
on shore rocks, clinging certain of soil and rain;
the stone whale, beached and buried; the weeds; the kelp;
the rock breakwater before me a path into the sea
in all its certainty; in my hand
a crow's feather, a pink shell
found broken for my sleeping friend.

Sun leaps from my fingers – the dusty scent
of skin in a web of light and salt
from the spill of the sea-spray

that seasons the air. Mist
rises from patches of sand like sails
pure as two white stones

we find to weigh our pockets.
We gather more, one dark with thin veins
like vapour trails, one sea-worn

red rich as blood. Then stop and lean
against a weathered log, the wind white,
bright and bitter cold.

We watch the waves surge over the pillars
of stone, urging themselves into the air
then rushing clear over the tide-smoothed sides

a spell that lulls us not to sleep
but to stay alone on the empty sands
to listen to the pull and scrape of stones

on stone, to watch the moon rise.
Then we've already climbed over the rocks
the logs, into the forest,

shed our clothes in the scratchy bracken,
in the chill night air
tasted the salt on each other's skin

and finally dressed again.
We walk together to the trail
the air rich with loam

years of falling cedar builds
and the hint of the bay already hidden
from view. With each rattle of wind

all salt and twigs, forest and sea
we are truly here. In my pocket
I finger a piece of driftwood

and a pine cone stolen
from the nest of this day.
This is how I want you

to remember me: salt and sun
warm on my skin, my hair
a thicket of cedar and moss,

laughing beside you along the trail,
counting our treasures, a shell,
a white stone that glows

pure and cold as sea or moon
but warm from our hold
counting our treasures, a handful of stones.

PLUM TREES

for Susan Robertson

In rain-scattered days
we pick summer fruit to preserve
and to trade in

like secrets. To cover
what hollows us
how the wind warms us

chills us, turning summer
to fall, quick sweetness
and nettles in twisting vines.

Last spring we sat here
as night fell, talking
to name our lives

to weave them a whole fabric
of love and grief.
Words spinning out

while the darkness
came slowly alight:
the tight buds

of the plum tree spread
into full open bloom.
The tree bursting alive.

Now its unpruned limbs
hang heavy with fruit –
and what we want is the life

we can tear from this tree:
all of it bitter and sweet –
lives woven of both,

of the words we shared
and allow to grow wild,
remembering the world

has more than one name
and one of those names
is joy.

My hands touch the water and I'm
crying. Simple as that.
I keep trying to put things together,
more than tears and water
while the sun, squeezed
between cloud and mountain,

focuses warm as a hand on my back.
I don't move. Wondering why the sky
opened like that, I see
myself in the water
with the sun behind and the dark
shape of the water nodding.

Nodding as if to tell me *yes*,
say *yes* to the man in the doorway
who has asked me to stay.
But it's not that simple, nothing is.
It's all too tangled

in years and the ways my body
knows his and knows nothing at all.
And it's this that I fear – the sun
setting over the mountain
like his mouth on my breast
and me wanting to push it

away, to run out into the street
naked, laughing.
It's too late to tell him lies.
The sun on my shoulder
is his hand and our motives are certain:
the parody of self

that is sometimes beauty.
The warm flesh. The fear
I want to name love.
I'm afraid I fall through life
and learn nothing – it is simple as that.
Simple to lift

my hands from the water
and turn to face into the sun.
And I would say simply
yes.

IV.   Against the Certain Grey

Overnight leave no bread on the table
and leave no milk: they draw back the dead − .

Rainer Maria Rilke, *Sonnets to Orpheus*

Take me away from the abstract –
if you talk about the earth
I want to sense the grit of soil
under my nails, feel
how it dries
the skin on my hands.
And love, don't talk of it
softly –
I want to know the way
it pulls down on you
from nowhere, everywhere,
one certain direction
like the cold rain.
I need to feel the way
it drives its chill right
into your bones.
Taste the tang of your fear
like metal on my tongue.
I beg you, no more considered
ponderous dreams. Promise me that.
Give me November, deep and sudden
in the turn of the year.
Rain and frost hone
the naked forest.
The wind's angry song
in the roof of the storm.
Dreams tangled and real
as war, as though ghosts
had awakened, gathered magic
in the dying days and growing
nights for their revenge,
their long fingers
at the door, tap tapping
with the rain, the scratch
of their nails along the shutters,

the twigs that break loose
from the trees to fly.
The wind's lull and battle,
thunder's roar and kettle's
rattle. Wind, rain, and the soul
eaten down to its bones, darkness.
And the warmth inside it. Cold
passion outside and a fire
within. You have told me this story
but I ask you, I need you
to tell me again.

stones slide beneath our feet
like waves falling from each other
february and rain blurs all horizons
melding sky and sea
our feet lose their hold
wherever we walk
where is your cold hand
your back before me is broad and dark
against the certain grey

between us more of the nameless
space that cannot help but remain
logs below us stumble
into each other with the push
and stutter of waves
my flesh is cold and naked
under the winter bulk of cloth
which wind and rain remove
thoughtless as passion
but with the same cold fingers, love

Night is a black beetle caught in my hair,
stars its million eyes.

If I were a child I'd squeeze its body
like warmed wax. I'm a woman who knows

ordinary men, the kind you might glance at
in passing, for their regular

defined beauty. The kind who
care for precision. A child

outside calls a lost animal, her voice
earnest as a bird's decoying cats

from the nest. Maybe it's her beetle I've stolen
and begun to dismember into its irregular

parts. In the street a deeper voice takes over.
If I were an animal I'd follow.

On my chest salamanders sleep
until they come near fire.

Salamanders stiffened by the breathing darkness
ordinary men leave you in. Even inside

your own room, with the night glued
against your windows, seeping through despite

all the candles you can ever burn.
This beetle uses the moon

for a scarred and frozen heart.
Night's beacon luring me to darkness,

a hole torn through to
those fires that must lie beyond.

Running through all those
days and nothing caught me
but the price of grain and
the odd book written or
burned. The weather was off.
Fruit trees bloomed in winter
and the locusts came, shedding wings
like angels. There were flames
in the sky and we lost
all urge to forecast. There was
no truth but that found
in the black belly of the streets
of the empty-throated town,
swallowing, swallowing. My lover
visited. Taking my arms he said
This is no apocalyptic dream.
But I knew that. I knew, too,
that there was much more we couldn't say
before he went east to exile
and did not return. He wore an
embroidered coat as he
waved out of the train, waved,
and our words were as little use
as locust wings. Planes
rode in like the times roaring,
each one a growl from the mountains,
moving out of hearing to stumble
into the sea. I had a nightmare of ladders,
rising, then bursting into flame
and crumbling above me. And the dust
was thick as dew, grinding
into our skins like glass
and it shone. We had run out
of time and virtues,
as in a child's bad dream

we have entered badly
like soldiers in hobnailed boots,
goose-stepping soldiers. We weren't
beginning and it wasn't
a dream, all sirens raising
the night and the sounds of engines
close by. We tried to
add it all up and got
merely sunrise. Try putting
that in a letter to someone
in exile. Try naming that.

Under the steel grey skies of Treblinka
the prisoners dig up rags to carry and burn.
They disintegrate in their hands
and the skeletal men are crying.
They keep working. The stiff evergreens behind them
are witness, stand guard to the secrets
of who knew what first, and what
caused who the greatest pain. They
are the grimmest trees I have ever seen.
The men keep moving; they cannot stop
even as I move through my ordinary life
in a city a world away. I watch them:
watch the wind rip through the thin cloth
of their flesh. The wind freezes tears
in eyes that can no longer watch
themselves. Mothers, children, daughters
and sons mean so little here they must
call them rags. Bitter rags the colour
of winter sky we try to hold them
in our hands. Carry them to be burned.
What does not burn must be crushed and emptied
into the river's arms. It can
hold them all better than we can –
we, whom knowledge makes thin,
whom knowledge turns into bitter
rags even in the shelter
of our ordinary lives.

> Ah, how lovely is the flower of anger,
> the red flower in my heart!

> First Fury, Sartre's *The Flies*

They have not run out of it yet, blood
or anger, they have plenty to paint

our faces with, write war across our cheeks,
broad stripes saying walk with them to battle.

The blood that burns scars so we never forget.

So what can we do? Nothing will turn their hands:
not words, not prayer, supplication won't move them

nor the tears that are our only balm, our healing.
Tears make *us* more human not them.

It is not enough to want an ending.

They will not leave us to gather whatever rags
we have and make of the tatters scant covering

to cloak us until the end, to keep our days empty
wondering what will change and what will change nothing.

I only know that speaking their names scalds them.

Embracing them our arms become their own
burning them as they would us. Hold them as I do

with whatever strength your life has left –
hold them against you, and with me say

I will not let you go except you bless me.

The pages I'd send you folded, discarded.
The phrases I've shaped in my mind for days
I don't dare send.
                            I begin this, dear friend:
and end, life is chancy enough, leave out
what's between. But begin again,
the scratch of the pen you gave me
another wound on white paper: dear friend:
and fail. Know my words can change nothing.

Trying once again, I ignore what I want to say;
say what I can. Write around myself,
faith in words to speak when I can't.

Diversions, a maze, leading you in.
Transcribe my stories to settle around you.

I believe in the common magic
of forests and household gods.

Once in a dream
I flew low and even with the ground,
below me crowds of animals I was leading
to safety, a new world. And my shadow,
my guide, was a tiger – what stirred his loping form
drew me.

A woman I know had a landlady in Greece
named Aphrodite. An old woman, her dusty
bones dressed in widow's weeds, her smile
naked as a rocky hill.
                        I believe in her,
love is like that.
                        And the visiting gardener
was named Agamemnon – twisted and old, still
a hero. Age is heroic. And common.
And bold.
I believe in the unexpected.

Approaching winter solstice, the year's night,
we keep reaching out in the dark solid air,
touch snow on the edge of the world.
We dream of this brightness, wake
cold with longing and sleep.

Herons in the mud are memory.
Lilith – the wife Adam had before the vengeful gods.
As though flame could be an entrance
into something other than flame.

I must try something else.
Another thread.

The Book of Common Knowledge is brown
its pages worn with the rub
of fingers that haven't touched it.
This is what we all know, no need for more.
So this book exists despite us,
telling us that knowledge is what we have
in common, that humans, like sparrows,
peck at their knowing with an unseeing
eye, alert only for danger, the weight
of thunder. Whatever may be distant
may be near.

It's never dark on the mountain in winter
snow reflects the moon reflects the sun,
holds light that is cold, clear.
No accident that ice is invisible and shines.
It's a different kind of drought from summer,
a different kind of drawing in. The fire
is all interior; there isn't time for speaking,
sharing the labyrinth of our thoughts and time.
We are solitary now, sleeping the clarity awake,
the cold wind that fires our cheeks.

The Book of Forgetting. Its spine is grey
and smells of water like a forest stream, moss and soil.
You ask it what is the colour of rain.
It says the colour of rain is the flavour
of stars: hidden, familiar. Still no closer
to an anecdote to the soul.

The golden architecture of dream
sometimes closes in,
                              a lover's voice
calling you, calling from outside
and you can't break through the walls,
although they're beautiful, portraits
carved out of the best days
of your life, days in the grass
by the lakeside, deep in the forest
in the heights of a tree, days that are
love returning. That voice –
you could hold it in your hands like a stone,
smooth and cool in your palm.
But what it says is your name
and the walls are all artifice
which renders them no less real.

The home of this imagination.
The border close but so difficult to cross
it might well be a foreign country.
You know your home by recognition
by all the familiar scents it has:
pine, wind, and the smell of trapped
dreams. Like a badger living in someone's
cabin doing all the damage only badgers
dream of. Don't try to catch one. It lives.

You find a bottled note on the shore
it says, *Find this here. This.*

Name every living forest you've seen,
it will be them all, the ordinary mist
of rain in the extraordinary forest.
The light is blessing,
liquid as ocean and quite as changeable.
It's the stream that stains your skin
with cedar and loosens your belly
and it dares you to drink.

Woman, I've seen you, reading
children's hands, pretending
to check that their palms are clean
while searching their lives.

In the morning there is nothing left.
The fieldstar has been burning
since dawn. As you walk the shoregrass
cuts you, and it doesn't matter.
It's only your blood
on the soil. I know this because
I know myself.

The tongue of the native speaker
is the language we were born to,
the words our tongue shaped
before we heard the world. What we said
to our mother's heart when we realized
we were hearing it. What we said
when we knew that it was all
something other – no need for words before
when all was ourselves. No need for
definition when there are no distinctions.

How we tease ourselves with these things.
Meaning how I tease myself
with these things.

Always the craftsman leaves a portion
of the work undone,
the sign pointing to God
but not naming him: myself. Describing
the void between what is and what
would be. The divorce between the idea
of *table* and the wood we know
and use daily.
                        So the scar livid
on perfect flesh. So the one unpainted
board beneath the eaves. So we can always
point to our objective and never say
that we have missed it, we may say
we're still reaching and
we will never sew the last button on.
As if the completion would undo us.

I can hear you say the words
I'd have you say to him.
Ah lover, thief of fire and dreams
I am what I was when we met
and now more.

Dear friend: life is chancy enough.

ACKNOWLEDGMENTS

I would like to thank the editors of the following magazines where these poems first appeared, sometimes in earlier versions:

THE ANTIGONISH REVIEW, *Crow Girl on Prairie in Elk's Tooth Dress; Aloysius Holds The Enemy; Crow Girl; Crow Girls Decorating Graves at Custer Battlefield* (as 'Four Crow Photographs')
ARC, Postcard of O'Keeffe
CALYX (U.S.A.), Lakeside Inventory
CANADIAN LITERATURE, High Water, Salamander Pendant, Saltspring, Swutlak Builds False Spring, White Lies
CONTEMPORARY VERSE 2, Hero at the Gates of Hell, Shoah
THE DALHOUSIE REVIEW, Electra to Orestes: Against the Furies, Into the Ravine (as 'What is the Poison Named?')
DANDELION, My Grandmother's Photograph
DESCANT, Settled in Montana for Winter
GRAIN, Fool's Gold on the Snow
THE GREENFIELD REVIEW (U.S.A.), Map of Vancouver Island
NEWEST, My Father Among the Mayans
NORTHERN LIGHTS (U.S.A.), *Four-Pole Crow Burial Scaffold; A Hillside in Spring*
POET LORE (U.S.A.), The Limits Undone (as 'Why I Would Think I am Leaving')
PRIMAVERA (U.S.A.), Midfire
QUARRY, Sea Glass from Execution Rock
QUEEN'S QUARTERLY, Berlin Dreams
WOT, Bird at Daybreak (as 'The Stolen Bird')

'Washing at Sunset' was a finalist in the 1990 National Poetry Contest and was published in *More Garden Varieties II*. 'September, New York' was a finalist in the 1993 contest and was published in *Vintage 1993*. 'Four-Pole Crow Burial Scaffold; A Hillside in Spring' was displayed with the exhibit, *Fred E. Miller: Photographer of the Crows*.

The italicized section in 'Sea Glass from Execution Rock' was borrowed from a letter by my mother, Shelagh Graham, and the italicized lines in 'High Water' from Pound's *Canto LXXXI*.

I would like to thank my family and friends for their stories, inspiration, and encouragement, especially Christina DeCoursey, Brenda Boeré, Shelagh & John Graham, Susan Robertson, Sylvia & Robin Skelton, and Bette Tomlinson. John Barton, Gail Dubrow, Richard Harrison, and Jim Gurley gave me invaluable help making these poems into a book. I would also like to thank John Donlan, Kitty Lewis, Sue Schenk, and Marnie Parsons of Brick Books for their editorial vision and their enthusiasm.

I am grateful to the Canada Council for a Project Grant, which enabled me to complete the poems and begin to shape this book.

Originally from Winnipeg, Manitoba, Neile Graham lived in British Columbia, Ontario, Washington State and western Montana during the ten years she spent writing the poems included in *Spells for Clear Vision*. Her poetry has appeared in such journals as *The Malahat Review*, *Grain*, *Mississippi Mud*, and *Northern Lights*. She has worked at universities, an alcoholic treatment centre, an astrophysical observatory, and a retail lumber & hardware company. Her previous work, *Seven Robins*, was published by Penumbra Press in 1983; she has also completed a children's novel, *Bryony's Needle*.